Pastoral Epistles: 1 Timothy, 2 Timothy, Titus

Pauline Epistles, Volume 5

Dr Andrew C S Koh

Published by Dr. Andrew C S Koh, 2022.

Copyright

Copyright © 2021 by Dr Andrew C S Koh

All rights reserved. No part of this book may be reproduced, stored in a retrieval system, or transmitted in any form or by any means, electronic, mechanical, photocopying, recording, or otherwise, without the prior written permission of the author, except for brief quotations embodied in critical articles or reviews. For information or permissions, please contact: Dr Andrew C S Koh andrewcskoh@duck.com

Cover design by Dr Andrew C S Koh Illustrations by Dr Andrew C S Koh

Unless otherwise stated, all Bible verses are quoted from The World English Bible

Scan the above QR code to get the free book

Unless otherwise quoted, all Scripture quotations are taken from the World English Bible, WEB.

Table of Contents

Foreword 1

Preface 3

Testimonials 4

Chapter 1 | Introduction to 1 Timothy 6

Chapter 2 | Salutation, Warning on Apostasy 8

Chapter 3 | World Evangelism, Christian Conduct 11

Chapter 4 | Selecting Overseers and Deacons 14

Chapter 5 | Apostasy, Doctrines, Spiritual Gifts 17

Chapter 6 | Care for Widows, Family, and Elders 20

Chapter 7 | Slaves, Masters, False Teachers, Love of Money 24

Chapter 8 | Introduction to 2 Timothy 28

Chapter 9 | Salutation, Prayer, Instructions 30

Chapter 10 | Pass the Baton of Faith 33

Chapter 11 | Apostasy, Heresy, Word of God 37

Chapter 12 | Farewell Address 40

Chapter 13 | Introduction to Titus 44

Chapter 14 | Salutation, Selecting Elders/ Bishops 46

Chapter 15 | Christian Relationships 49

Chapter 16 | Farewell Address 52

About the Author 55

One Last Thing 57

To my beloved wife, Wai Yin, whose love and unwavering support have been the foundation of everything I do.

To my sons, who have brought joy and purpose into my life.

To my daughters-in-law, who have enriched our family with their warmth and kindness.

To my grandsons and granddaughters, the light of my life, who remind me daily of the beauty and wonder of the world.

Above all, to the glory of God, whose grace has guided me through every step of my journey.

Finally, this book is for you.

"Fight the good fight of the faith. Take hold of the eternal life to which you were called," 1 Timothy 6:12

Foreword

Paul's pastoral letters are, as good as, his last testament. He knew his time was coming to an end soon. With his final exhortation to his disciples, he continued to press home the point to be faithful to Christ, as he himself had been throughout his ministry. What a great and amazing disciple of Christ Paul was, one who, irrespective of the terrible treatments he had received from his persecutors and the enemies of the Gospel yet could say that I have fought the good fight, I have finished the race, I have kept the faith.

Paul, too, did not deliberately only say the nice things to present a good picture of himself and his ministry. He was very firm with right theological understanding as well as proper and holy living. So, he did not mince his words to lash out at those who taught heretical doctrines and those who practised immoral and impure living. He recognized that the churches had been infiltrated with many worldly influences and traditions. Thus, he strongly condemned the inconsistent and improper elements that had existed in the churches that caused divisions and destroyed good testimonies. He encouraged his beloved disciples Timothy and Titus to return to teach the redemptive work of Christ (according to His mercy He saved us, through the washing of regeneration and renewing of the Holy Spirit, through Jesus Christ our Savior, that having been justified by His grace we should become heirs according to the hope of eternal life) and to live lives of Christlikeness as heirs of God, as well as to appoint bishops and elders to do likewise.

The author has pinpointed affirmatively that there is no place for discrimination in the service of God and laxity in the proper understanding of the theology and gospel of Christ, as well as in the selection of church leadership. May the good Lord have mercy upon us and grant us His wisdom and understanding always.

Archbishop Ng Moon Hing, Anglican Archbishop of Southeast Asia, 2021

DR ANDREW C S KOH

Preface

Grow in your knowledge and grace of our Lord and Savior Jesus Christ with Dr. Andrew C. S. Koh's *Pastoral Epistles*. This book provides an expositional Bible study and devotional guide on 1 Timothy, 2 Timothy, and Titus. Through careful reading, study, meditation, and application of Scripture, readers will gain a better understanding of the late writings of the apostle Paul.

Koh has given a clear background and simple explanations of every passage in 1 Timothy, 2 Timothy, and Titus. These epistles have important teachings on pastoral leadership, Christian conduct and relationships, countering heretical teachers and early Gnosticism, which are still very applicable to our modern church today. At the end of each lesson, he gives a devotional application and prayer.

With the help of this study guide readers will gain a comprehensive and foundational understanding of 1 Timothy, 2 Timothy, and Titus. It is perfect for students of the Bible who are looking to deepen their knowledge of these epistles.

If you are looking to grow in the knowledge and grace of our Lord and Savior Jesus Christ, Dr. Andrew C. S. Koh's *Pastoral Epistles* will get you started on your journey.

Dr. Andrew C. S. Koh, 2021

Testimonials

These books hold a special place for me in my heart. I enjoy reading about "rules" and reasons behind said rules. These books tell just that. If you enjoy reading about the consequences and organizational structure of hierarchy then these books will leave you wanting more, T Townsend.

1 Timothy, 2 Timothy, Titus by Dr. Andrew C S Koh is a great way to study the Letters of Timothy (1 and 2) and Titus. I found the book to be a great study guide and a great time to reflect on myself. I would recommend this book to anyone wanting a deeper understanding of Faith that is found in the Books of 1 Timothy, 2 Timothy, and Titus, Kevin Booker.

1 Timothy, 2 Timothy, Titus are the letters written by Paul. Paul believed in saying the truth. He knew his past and had no problem admitting his own sins. He did not mince words. He saw that many of the churches were being influenced by outside sources. He called his beloved disciples, Timothy and Titus, to return to teach the redemptive work of Christ. Paul felt need for proper understanding of the theology and Gospel of Christ, as well as in the selection of church leadership. He felt that there were those in power in the churches that were leading their flocks astray. He asks us to look at our own leaders and to know that there are many false teachers and prophets who preach and teach corrupt doctrines today, PAR.

A great read and very informative. The advice of Apostle Paul to Timothy about how to lead a good Christian life. A very practical book. This is my honest review, Sharmani Jeyaram.

I love these books by Dr. Andrew C S Koh! He breaks down each part of the Bible into short pieces so that people can see things in the Bible that they would not have known on their first reading. This book is truly engaging, Rowan E Creech.

Chapter 1

Introduction to 1 Timothy

Prayer

Heavenly Father, we acknowledge that You are Almighty God, God of creation, God of salvation, God of redemption, and God of reconciliation. We pray for divine inspiration, understanding, insight, and enablement to understand and apply Your Word. In Jesus' name, amen.

Author, Place, Date, Purpose, and Recipients

Paul wrote a personal letter to Timothy to encourage, warn, and instruct him. He penned this letter from Macedonia between AD 62 to 64 after being released from his first Roman imprisonment. Timothy was Paul's protégé, spiritual son, and pastor of the Ephesian church.

This is one of three pastoral epistles: 1 Timothy, 2 Timothy, and Titus. Ephesus was a Roman port city in Asia Minor (modern-day Turkey) and was home to the temple of Diana or Artemis. False teachers who prohibited marriage and eating of certain foods had infiltrated the Ephesian church.

Themes

Some of the themes are false doctrines, holiness, godliness, prayer, world evangelism, Christian conduct in worship, qualifications of church leaders, and Christian relationships.

Outline

1 Timothy 1:1–20, salutation, warning on apostasy

1 Timothy 2:1–2:16, instructions on prayer, evangelism, and Christian conduct

1 Timothy 3:1–14, criteria for selecting overseers and deacons

1 Timothy 4:1–16, warning on apostasy, teaching sound doctrine, exercising spiritual gifts

1 Timothy 5:1–25, Christian relationships, care for widows, family, elders

1 Timothy 6:1–21, slaves, masters, warning against false teachers and the love of money

Application

Paul's letter to Timothy offers advice and guidance on church leadership, doctrine and godly behavior. Paul gave advice on how to maintain church order while living according to Christian beliefs in everyday life.

Paul emphasized the importance of sound doctrine and the qualifications for church leaders, including overseers and deacons. Additionally, Paul encouraged us to persevere in his faith despite challenges and to confront false teachings.

We should cultivate a spirit of love and faithfulness within the church community and to treat others with kindness and respect, showing the example of Christ's unconditional love. We should be strong in evangelism to spread the gospel.

Paul should reject false teachers, pray, and conduct ourselves properly in church worship. We should adhere to the criteria for choosing church leaders as spelled out by Paul.

Prayer

Heavenly Father, thank You that we can study the epistle of 1 Timothy. Open our eyes and ears as we study holy Scripture. Open our understanding to explore the riches of Your Word. We pray for insight into controversial passages. In Jesus' name, amen.

Chapter 2
Salutation, Warning on Apostasy

1 Timothy 1:1–20

Verses 1–2, *1 Paul, an apostle of Jesus Christ according to the commandment of God our Savior and the Lord Jesus Christ our hope; 2 to Timothy, my true child in faith: Grace, mercy, and peace, from God our Father and Christ Jesus our Lord.*

Reflection

Paul was called to be an apostle authorized by God and the Lord Jesus Christ. Greek for "apostle" is *apostolos*, which means ambassador or emissary. Greek for "commandment" is *epitage*, which means authority. Paul was an ambassador of Christ, our Savior and hope, by the authority of God. Paul wrote this epistle to Timothy, his protégé, and spiritual son in the faith. He pronounced to Timothy a blessing of grace, mercy, and peace from God, our Father, and the Lord Jesus Christ, our Lord.

Verses 3–4, *3 As I urged you when I was going into Macedonia, stay at Ephesus that you might command certain men not to teach a different doctrine, 4 and not to pay attention to myths and endless genealogies, which cause disputes, rather than God's stewardship, which is in faith.*

Reflection

When Paul was in Macedonia, he encouraged Timothy to stay back in Ephesus because false teachers had infiltrated the Ephesian church with false doctrines, myths, and disputable genealogies.

Verses 5–7, *5 but the goal of this command is love, out of a pure heart and a good conscience and sincere faith, 6 from which things some, having missed the mark, have turned away to vain talking, 7 desiring to be teachers of the law, though they understand neither what they say, nor about what they strongly affirm.*

Reflection

Paul encouraged Timothy to love with a pure heart, good conscience, and sincere faith. Paul warned him about legalistic teachers who were ignorant of the law.

Verses 8–11, *8 But we know that the law is good, if a person uses it lawfully, 9 as knowing this, that law is not made for a righteous person, but for the lawless and insubordinate, for the ungodly and sinners, for the unholy and profane, for murderers of fathers and murderers of mothers, for manslayers, 10 for the sexually immoral, for homosexuals, for slave-traders, for liars, for perjurers, and for any other thing contrary to the sound doctrine, 11 according to the Good News of the glory of the blessed God, which was committed to my trust.*

Reflection

The law is good but people are carnal and cannot keep the law. The law was not made for the righteous but for sinners, murderers, sexual perverts, kidnappers, liars, and so on. The law convicts people that they are sinners who need a Savior. The law is the mirror that reflects and reveals sin. The law is a schoolmaster to point people to Christ.

Verses 12–14, *12 I thank him who enabled me, Christ Jesus our Lord, because he counted me faithful, appointing me to service; 13 although I used to be a blasphemer, a persecutor, and insolent. However, I obtained mercy, because I did it ignorantly in unbelief. 14 The grace of our Lord abounded exceedingly with faith and love which is in Christ Jesus.*

Reflection

Greek for "insolent" is *hybrizo*, which means violent. Paul thanks the Lord for His superabundant love, mercy, and grace to appoint him as an apostle even though he was once a blasphemer, a persecutor of Christians, and a violent man.

Verses 15–17, *15 The saying is faithful and worthy of all acceptance, that Christ Jesus came into the world to save sinners, of whom I am chief. 16 However, for this cause I obtained mercy, that in me first, Jesus Christ might display all his patience for an example of those who were going to believe in him for eternal life. 17 Now to the King eternal, immortal, invisible, to God who alone is wise, be honor and glory forever and ever. Amen.*

Reflection

Christ came to earth to save sinners by grace and through faith. Paul called himself the chief of sinners. Greek for "long-suffering" is *makrothymia*, which means patience, Christ is a God of love, grace, mercy, and patience. In doxology, Paul proclaimed Christ as the eternal King, who is immortal, invisible, wise, honorable, and glorious.

Verses 18–20, *18 I commit this instruction to you, my child Timothy, according to the prophecies which were given to you before, that by them you may wage the good warfare, 19 holding faith and a good conscience, which some having thrust away made a shipwreck concerning the faith, 20 of whom are Hymenaeus and Alexander, whom I delivered to Satan, that they might be taught not to blaspheme.*

Reflection

Greek for "charge" is *parangellia*, which means a military order. Paul ordered Timothy to fight the good fight against false teachers with faith and a good conscience. Paul singled out two false teachers and blasphemers by name, Hymenaeus and Alexander.

Application

Assess the sources of spiritual learning. Are you selective in what teachings and practices you adopt and pass on to others?

Will you study the Bible regularly with reliable teachers to ensure you fully understand its doctrine?

Will you ensure that any information you share with others is aligned with biblical truth?

Spiritual growth is dependent on the study of the Bible and finding trustworthy teachers. As part of your journey, it is important to ensure that the information you provide aligns with Biblical truth.

Know the truth by studying Scripture diligently and the truth shall set us free from deception. Christ came to earth to save sinners by grace through faith in Him.

Love out of a pure heart, good conscience, and sincere faith. Discern and reject false doctrines and false teachers by having a good basic knowledge of Scripture.

Prayer

Heavenly Father, thank You for the truth of Your Word that transcends time, culture, geography, race, and history. We pray for Your Word to be deeply imprinted into our hearts. We pray for divine enablement, understanding, and application. In Jesus' name, amen.

Chapter 3
World Evangelism, Christian Conduct

1 Timothy 2:1–15

Verses 1–4, *1 I exhort therefore, first of all, that petitions, prayers, intercessions, and giving of thanks be made for all men: 2 for kings and all who are in high places, that we may lead a tranquil and quiet life in all godliness and reverence. 3 For this is good and acceptable in the sight of God our Savior, 4 who desires all people to be saved and come to full knowledge of the truth.*

Reflection

Prayers should be offered for all people, including kings and leaders in authority so that there will be peace, reverence for God, and godliness in the community. There are four kinds of prayers: supplications, prayers, intercessions, and thanksgiving. Greek for "supplication" is *deesis*, which means a specific request concerning a person's own needs. Greek for "prayer" is *proseuche*, which means a general request. Greek for "intercession" is *enteuxis*, which means a specific request concerning the needs of others. Greek for "thanksgiving" is *eucharistia*, which means gratitude. God desires world evangelism and salvation for all people.

Verses 5–7, *5 For there is one God, and one mediator between God and men, the man Christ Jesus, 6 who gave himself as a ransom for all, the testimony in its own times, 7 to which I was appointed a preacher and an apostle—I am telling the truth in Christ, not lying—a teacher of the Gentiles in faith and truth.*

Reflection

There is one God and Jesus Christ is the mediator between God and people. When He died on the cross at Calvary and rose from the dead, Christ removed the wall that separated God from people. Now we can come to God with confidence through the blood of Christ and in the name of Christ. We do not need to go before a human high priest to confess our sins.

Greek for "ransom" is *lytron*, which means a payment to procure freedom for a slave. Christ gave Himself as payment to procure our freedom from slavery to sin by dying on the cross as the perfect Lamb of God. Paul preached and taught the truth of the gospel of Christ to the Gentiles.

Verse 8, *I desire therefore that the men in every place pray, lifting up holy hands without anger and doubting.*

Reflection

Greek for "holy" is *hosios*, which means godly, pious, or righteous. Greek for "wrath" is *orge*, which means anger. Holy hands are hands that are pious, righteous, and godly. The posture of prayer is to raise righteous and faithful hands in surrender and submission to God.

Verses 9–12, *9 In the same way, that women also adorn themselves in decent clothing, with modesty and propriety, not just with braided hair, gold, pearls, or expensive clothing, 10 but with good works, which is appropriate for women professing godliness. 11 Let a woman learn in quietness with full submission. 12 But I don't permit a woman to teach, nor to exercise authority over a man, but to be in quietness.*

Reflection

Women should dress modestly and in moderation avoiding extensive make-up, wearing expensive clothes and jewelry. Compare 1 Timothy 6:5–10. The women should submit to male authority in public places of worship: compare 1 Timothy 5:11–15. Paul's prohibition for a woman to teach in the church is not a universal command for all people of all times. This is a cultural command for the first-century world when women were not educated. In that culture, it was appropriate for women not to teach or lead a congregation. Today women are educated and knowledgeable in every profession and this prohibition does not apply. Society and culture in the first-century world were not the same as our modern twenty-first-century world.

Verses 13–15, *13 For Adam was formed first, then Eve. 14 Adam wasn't deceived, but the woman, being deceived, has fallen into disobedience; 15 but she will be saved through her childbearing, if they continue in faith, love, and sanctification with sobriety.*

Reflection

God created Adam first, not Eve. Satan deceived Eve, not Adam. This is an allusion to Genesis 3:15.

Genesis 3:15, *To the woman he said, "I will make your pains in childbearing very severe; with painful labor, you will give birth to children. Your desire will be for your husband, and he will rule over you."*

Application

Check the quality of your prayers. How often do you pray for others? Regular prayer is important for you and those around you, including community leaders and politicians who lead nations and communities. This can help develop compassion and intercession for people in power.

Regular prayer is important for your own well-being, as well as for the well-being of your community and nation. Prioritizing intercession can foster compassion and empathy, and create a spirit of support and solidarity within society.

Pray with supplications, for your own needs, pray generally for all needs, intercede for other people's needs out of a heart of gratitude to God in an appropriate posture of submission.

Evangelize others in response to the great commission. Women should dress modestly in public places of worship.

Prohibition for women to teach or lead in church may not be applicable to the twenty-first-century world.

Prayer

Heavenly Father, thank You for instructions on prayer, evangelism, and Christian conduct in worship. We pray for the anointing of the Holy Spirit, and divine enablement to share the gospel of Christ to our family, relatives, friends, and contacts. Help us to apply Scripture in our daily lives. In Jesus' name, amen.

Chapter 4
Selecting Overseers and Deacons

Prayer

Heavenly Father, we pray for the anointing of the Holy Spirit to help us in the exegesis and hermeneutics of Scripture. We pray for wisdom in unlocking the meaning of controversial and difficult passages. In Jesus' name, amen.

1 Timothy 3:1–16

Verses 1–7, 1 This is a faithful saying: someone who seeks to be an overseer desires a good work. 2 The overseer therefore must be without reproach, the husband of one wife, temperate, sensible, modest, hospitable, good at teaching; 3 not a drinker, not violent, not greedy for money, but gentle, not quarrelsome, not covetous; 4 one who rules his own house well, having children in subjection with all reverence; 5 (but how could someone who doesn't know how to rule one's own house take care of God's assembly?) 6 not a new convert, lest being puffed up he fall into the same condemnation as the devil. 7 Moreover he must have good testimony from those who are outside, to avoid falling into reproach and the snare of the devil.

Reflection

Greek for bishop is *episkopos*, which means overseer. A bishop must have a desire for the position. Greek for sober-minded is *nepho*, which means not intoxicated by wine. Paul spelled out the criteria required for selecting a bishop.

He must be without reproach, monogamous, self-controlled, not intoxicated by wine, of good character, hospitable, have teaching capability, be gentle, abstain from wine, not be violent, not be greedy for money, and not be covetous.

He must show good family leadership with his children having a good character. He must have a good testimony among non-believers and must not be a novice in the Christian faith.

Verses 8–13, 8 Servants, in the same way, must be reverent, not double-tongued, not addicted to much wine, not greedy for money, 9 holding the mystery of the faith in a pure conscience. 10 Let them also first be tested; then let them serve if they are blameless. 11 Their wives in the same way must be reverent, not slanderers, temperate, and faithful in all things. 12 Let servants be husbands of one wife, ruling their children and their own houses well. 13 For those who have served well gain for themselves a good standing, and great boldness in the faith which is in Christ Jesus.

Reflection

Greek for deacon is *diakonos*, which means servant. Greek for double tongue is *dilogos*, which means to be deceitful. Greek for slanderer is *diabolos*, which means backbiter. Paul listed the criteria for selecting a deacon. He must be respectable, not deceitful, not a drunkard, not greedy for money, and have a pure conscience. Their wives must be respectable, not a backbiter, self-controlled, and faithful. Deacons must be monogamous and have raised their families beyond reproach.

Verses 14–16, *14 These things I write to you, hoping to come to you shortly; 15 but if I wait long, that you may know how men ought to behave themselves in God's house, which is the assembly of the living God, the pillar and ground of the truth. 16 Without controversy, the mystery of godliness is great: God was revealed in the flesh, justified in the spirit, seen by angels, preached among the nations, believed on in the world, and received up in glory.*

Reflection

Paul hoped to visit Timothy soon. He encouraged Timothy to conduct himself above reproach in godliness in the church of the living God. Jesus is God manifested in the flesh through the incarnation. He was justified by the Holy Spirit, seen by angels, preached to the Gentiles, believed by the world, and ascended to heaven in glory.

Application

Examine your integrity and character carefully. Both are essential to building trust in every area of your life. Are you a leader in your community who meets biblical standards? Develop qualities like self-control and hospitality, regardless of the formal leadership position you hold.

Leadership is more than just a position. It's about how you affect others. You can influence change in your community by demonstrating self-control, remaining loyal and being welcoming. This will lead to personal growth as well as positive changes for everyone involved.

To be a successful and influential leader, you must demonstrate these qualities. Leading by example and embodying these qualities are key components to effective leadership.

Paul spelled out very strict criteria for selecting bishops/elders and deacons. These leaders must conduct themselves above reproach in godliness. Congregations must follow these criteria when selecting people into these positions.

Jesus is God manifested in the flesh, fully God and fully man. He died, was buried, rose, was glorified, ascended to heaven, and will return to earth again at His second coming.

Prayer

Heavenly Father, thank You for spelling out the criteria for selecting bishops/elders and deacons of the church. We pray for divine enablement to live godly lives beyond reproach as we await the second coming of our Lord and Savior Jesus Christ. In Jesus' name, amen.

Chapter 5
Apostasy, Doctrines, Spiritual Gifts

1 Timothy 4:1–16

Verses 1–5, *1 But the Spirit says expressly that in later times some will fall away from the faith, paying attention to seducing spirits and doctrines of demons, 2 through the hypocrisy of men who speak lies, branded in their own conscience as with a hot iron, 3 forbidding marriage and commanding to abstain from foods which God created to be received with thanksgiving by those who believe and know the truth. 4 For every creature of God is good, and nothing is to be rejected, if it is received with thanksgiving. 5 For it is sanctified through the word of God and prayer.*

Reflection

Greek for 'depart from the faith' is *apostasia*, which means apostasy. In the last days, some Christians will become apostate, believing in demonic spirits, false doctrines, and lies with hypocrisy and a hardened conscience. Against the teaching of biblical truth, these heretical teachers prohibited marriage and eating of certain foods.

Verses 6–11, *6 If you instruct the brothers of these things, you will be a good servant of Christ Jesus, nourished in the words of the faith, and of the good doctrine which you have followed. 7 But refuse profane and old wives' fables. Exercise yourself toward godliness. 8 For bodily exercise has some value, but godliness has value in all things, having the promise of the life which is now, and of that which is to come. 9 This saying is faithful and worthy of all acceptance. 10 For to this end we both labor and suffer reproach, because we have set our trust in the living God, who is the Savior of all men, especially of those who believe. 11 Command and teach these things.*

Reflection

Paul instructed Timothy as a minister of Christ to nourish Christians with sound doctrines based on biblical truth, rejecting myths and old wives' tales. Physical exercise is good for physical health but the advantage is only temporal.

Spiritual exercise, on the other hand, is good for spiritual health and the advantage is eternal. To this end, Paul labored and suffered persecutions. God is the living God and Savior of all people who believe.

Verses 12–16, *12 Let no man despise your youth; but be an example to those who believe, in word, in your way of life, in love, in spirit, in faith, and in purity. 13 Until I come, pay attention to reading, to exhortation, and to teaching. 14 Don't neglect the gift that is in you, which was given to you by prophecy, with the laying on of the hands of the elders. 15 Be diligent in these things. Give yourself wholly to them, that your progress may be revealed to all. 16 Pay attention to yourself and to your teaching. Continue in these things, for in doing this you will save both yourself and those who hear you.*

Reflection

Paul encouraged Timothy not to feel inferior because of his youth, and to be a role model for Christians through good conduct, love, spirituality, faithfulness, and purity of heart. Paul instructed Timothy to read, study, encourage, teach the word of truth, and exercise spiritual gifts imparted to him by the elders through the laying of hands. Timothy was to meditate on Scripture and teach the doctrines to save himself and those who heard him.

Application

Reflect on your spiritual practices. Are you committed to strengthening godliness by prayer, scripture reading, and worship? Create a regular spiritual practice routine with the goal of growing godliness by putting in intentional effort.

Strengthen your connection with the Lord by establishing a daily routine that incorporates spiritual practices. Spiritual disciplines can transform your inner life. Be determined and mindful in your pursuit.

You will be able to face the challenges of life if you engage in these practices. You will not only experience a greater sense of godliness, but also a profound sense of peace and fulfillment.

Do not fall away from the faith of heretical teachings. Discern false doctrines by being biblically literate. Spend time studying Scripture diligently and regularly.

The Bible has 1,189 chapters. By reading four chapters a day, you will cover the whole Bible in 300 days. I encourage you to start today. If you are biblically literate, no one can deceive you.

Prayer

Heavenly Father, we acknowledge that You are the Lord, God Almighty. We confess that we were sinners and are now saved by Your grace. We thank You for all that You have done for us in our lives. We pray for protection, and good health. In Jesus' name, amen.

Chapter 6
Care for Widows, Family, and Elders

1 Timothy 5:1–25

Verses 1–2, *1 Don't rebuke an older man, but exhort him as a father; the younger men as brothers; 2 the elder women as mothers; the younger as sisters, in all purity.*

Reflection

Paul instructed Timothy to respect older men as fathers, younger men as brothers, older women as mothers, and, with a pure heart, younger women as sisters in Christ.

Verses 3–7, *3 Honor widows who are widows indeed. 4 But if any widow has children or grandchildren, let them learn first to show piety toward their own family and to repay their parents, for this is acceptable in the sight of God. 5 Now she who is a widow indeed and desolate, has her hope set on God, and continues in petitions and prayers night and day. 6 But she who gives herself to pleasure is dead while she lives. 7 Also command these things, that they may be without reproach.*

Reflection

Paul instructed Timothy to honor widows who had no children and were faithful to God in prayers and supplications and to support them with welfare. Widows who had children should be looked after by their children. Paul rebuked widows who indulged in the pleasures of life. Widows should remain above reproach in their conduct.

Verses 8–10, *8 But if anyone doesn't provide for his own, and especially his own household, he has denied the faith, and is worse than an unbeliever. 9 Let no one be enrolled as a widow under sixty years old, having been the wife of one man, 10 being approved by good works, if she has brought up children, if she has been hospitable to strangers, if she has washed the saints' feet, if she has relieved the afflicted, and if she has diligently followed every good work.*

Reflection

Christians should take care of their family members. Younger widows under 60 years of age should not be added to the welfare list, unless they were monogamous, had a good reputation in the community, had raised children, received strangers, served Christians, helped the afflicted, and were diligent in good works.

Verses 11–16, *11 But refuse younger widows, for when they have grown wanton against Christ, they desire to marry, 12 having condemnation, because they have rejected their first pledge. 13 Besides, they also learn to be idle, going about from house to house. Not only idle, but also gossips and busybodies, saying things which they ought not. 14 I desire therefore that the younger widows marry, bear children, rule the household, and give no occasion to the adversary for insulting. 15 For already some have turned away after Satan. 16 If any man or woman who believes has widows, let them relieve them, and don't let the assembly be burdened, that it might relieve those who are widows indeed.*

Reflection

Paul gave specific instructions regarding how to treat younger widows. Paul warned against these widows into the church's support system because of idleness and gossip. Instead, he encouraged these women to marry, have kids, and manage their household independently.

Christians who have widows in their household, should look after them and not burden the church.

Verses 17–18, *17 Let the elders who rule well be counted worthy of double honor, especially those who labor in the word and in teaching. 18 For the Scripture says, "You shall not muzzle the ox when it treads out the grain. [Deuteronomy 25:4]" And, "The laborer is worthy of his wages. [Leviticus 19:13; Luke 10:7]"*

Reflection

Greek for elder is *presbyteros*, which means an elder of a Christian church. *Presbyteros* is similar to *episkopos*, which means bishop or overseer. Elders who teach the Bible should be honored and remunerated accordingly.

Verses 19–20, *19 Don't receive an accusation against an elder, except at the word of two or three witnesses. 20 Those who sin, reprove in the sight of all, that the rest also may be in fear.*

Reflection

Any accusation against an elder must be supported by two or three witnesses. As a deterrent to others, Paul instructed Timothy to rebuke in the presence of everyone those who had sinned.

Verses 21–22, *21 I command you in the sight of God, and the Lord Jesus Christ, and the chosen angels, that you observe these things without prejudice, doing nothing by partiality. 22 Lay hands hastily on no one. Don't be a participant in other people's sins. Keep yourself pure.*

Reflection

Paul instructed Timothy to observe these things without any bias or favoritism. Paul instructed Timothy not to take action on anyone in haste and to keep himself pure.

Verses 23–25, *23 Be no longer a drinker of water only, but use a little wine for your stomach's sake and your frequent infirmities. 24 Some men's sins are evident, preceding them to judgment, and some also follow later. 25 In the same way also there are good works that are obvious, and those that are otherwise can't be hidden.*

Reflection

Paul instructed Timothy to drink a little wine for his stomach's ailment and other frequent illnesses. Paul told Timothy to discern between sinful and good people.

Application

Assess your interactions with others. You should treat each person with honor and respect. Treat the members of your church community with kindness and consideration.

Instead of criticizing others, try to encourage them with words of support and kindness. This will create a community where everyone feels valued and respected.

In order to create a sense of belonging and unity, it is important that you set an example. Paul's advice will empower and uplift each member of your congregation, further cementing the bonds.

This will ultimately strengthen the church community and foster a culture of love and compassion. Encouraging and supporting each other is essential for building a strong and connected congregation.

We should respect the elderly, young adults, widows, family members, and spiritual teachers of the Word. We should look after the welfare of our family members and others who require support without bias. There will be plenty of opportunities to apply this teaching in life.

Prayer

Heavenly Father, we pray for mercy, grace, and forgiveness of sin. We confess that we have sinned against You. We stand in the gap to intercede for our family, friends, and colleagues. In Jesus' name, amen.

Chapter 7
Slaves, Masters, False Teachers, Love of Money

1 Timothy 6:1–21

Verses 1–2, *1 Let as many as are bondservants under the yoke count their own masters worthy of all honor, that the name of God and the doctrine not be blasphemed. 2 Those who have believing masters, let them not despise them because they are brothers, but rather let them serve them, because those who partake of the benefit are believing and beloved. Teach and exhort these things.*

Reflection

Christians who were slaves should honor their masters, particularly if they were Christians. Christians who were slaves should serve their Christian masters as brothers in Christ.

Verses 3–5, *3 If anyone teaches a different doctrine, and doesn't consent to sound words, the words of our Lord Jesus Christ, and to the doctrine which is according to godliness, 4 he is conceited, knowing nothing, but obsessed with arguments, disputes, and word battles, from which come envy, strife, insulting, evil suspicions, 5 constant friction of people of corrupt minds and destitute of the truth, who suppose that godliness is a means of gain. Withdraw yourself from such.*

Reflection

Paul warned Timothy to reject pedlars of heretical Gnostic doctrines, who were proud, ignorant, argumentative, envious, aggressive, abusive, evil, corrupt, deceptive, greedy, and misused the gospel for financial gain.

Verses 6–10, *6 But godliness with contentment is great gain. 7 For we brought nothing into the world, and we certainly can't carry anything out. 8 But having food and clothing, we will be content with that. 9 But those who are determined to be rich fall into a temptation, a snare, and many foolish and harmful lusts, such as drown men in ruin and destruction. 10 For the love of money is a root of all kinds of evil. Some have been led astray from the faith in their greed, and have pierced themselves through with many sorrows.*

Reflection

Godliness and contentment are great Christian virtues to embrace. Everyone entered the world without anything and will leave the world without anything.

Everyone should be content to have the necessities of life such as food and clothing. Anyone who desires to get rich falls into the temptation of sin and destroys themselves. All the evils of the world are due to money greediness and not to money *per se.*

Verses 11–12, *11 But you, man of God, flee these things, and follow after righteousness, godliness, faith, love, perseverance, and gentleness. 12 Fight the good fight of faith. Take hold of the eternal life to which you were called, and you confessed the good confession in the sight of many witnesses.*

Reflection

Addressing Timothy as a man of God, Paul encouraged him to pursue righteousness, godliness, faithfulness, love, patience, and gentleness. These are some of the fruit of the Spirit, Galatians 5:22–23. Paul encouraged Timothy to fight the good fight of faith and claim the promise of eternal life.

Galatians 5:22–23, *But the fruit of the Spirit is love, joy, peace, longsuffering, kindness, goodness, faithfulness, gentleness, self-control. Against such there is no law.*

Verses 13–16, *13 I command you before God, who gives life to all things, and before Christ Jesus, who before Pontius Pilate testified the good confession, 14 that you keep the commandment without spot, blameless, until the appearing of our Lord Jesus Christ, 15 which in its own times he will show, who is the blessed and only Ruler, the King of kings, and Lord of lords. 16 He alone has immortality, dwelling in unapproachable light, whom no man has seen, nor can see: to whom be honor and eternal power. Amen.*

Reflection

Paul urged Timothy before the creator God and Jesus Christ as his witnesses to keep Christ's commandments above reproach until His second coming. Greek for "potentate" is *dynastes,* which means prince. Verse 15 is a doxology. Jesus Christ, the Prince, King of kings, and Lord of lords is immortal, glorious, and invisible, who has the honor and everlasting power.

Verses 17–19, *17 Charge those who are rich in this present world that they not be arrogant, nor have their hope set on the uncertainty of riches, but on the living God, who richly provides us with everything to enjoy; 18 that they do good, that they be rich in good works, that they be ready to distribute, willing to share; 19 laying up in store for themselves a good foundation against the time to come, that they may lay hold of eternal life. Grace be with you. Amen.*

Reflection

Those who are rich in this present life should not be proud and trust in uncertain riches but in the living God. They should be rich in doing good works, generous, and willing to share to store up for themselves treasures in heaven.

Matthew 6:19–20, *Do not store up for yourselves treasures on earth, where moths and vermin destroy, and where thieves break in and steal. But store up for yourselves treasures in heaven, where moths and vermin do not destroy, and where thieves do not break in and steal.*

Reflection

Verses 20–21, *20 Timothy, guard that which is committed to you, turning away from the empty chatter and oppositions of what is falsely called knowledge, 21 which some profess, and thus have wandered from the faith.*

Reflection

Paul instructed Timothy to avoid blasphemy, foolish talking, and false doctrines that will lead Christians away from the faith. Paul pronounced a blessing of grace on Timothy.

Application

Be grateful for the things you have and be generous to others. Practice gratitude rather than longing for something more. Find ways to share resources generously with those who are in need.

By being grateful for what you have, you can cultivate a positive mindset and bring joy into your life. Sharing resources with others in need can spread kindness and make a meaningful impact in their lives.

Consider carefully how you will protect your faith. Stay vigilant in protecting your faith from false teachings, distractions, and other influences that may tempt you to stray from it.

Surround yourself with supportive like-minded individuals who can help you stay focused and grounded in your faith. Regularly seeking spiritual guidance and deepening your faith can help you protect and overcome challenges.

Treat your employers with respect; especially if they are Christians. Reject pedlars of heretical doctrines. Embrace godliness with contentment. Stay away from pride, materialism, and money greediness. Avoid blasphemy and foolish talk.

Prayer

Heavenly Father, thank You for this timely message on the employee–employer relationship, heresy, and correct handling of money. We pray for wisdom to understand and apply Paul's instructions to Timothy to our lives, as these instructions transcend time and culture. In Jesus' name, amen.

Chapter 8

Introduction to 2 Timothy

Prayer

Heavenly Father, we pray for You to speak to us to convict, correct, encourage, and train us in godly and righteous living. We pray for the divine transformation of hearts, renewal of minds, and the ability to discern Your good and perfect will. In Jesus' name, amen.

Author, Date, Recipient, Setting

After Paul's release from his first Roman imprisonment in AD 62, he visited old churches and planted new ones in Macedonia and Asia Minor. He was rearrested by the Romans in AD 66 and thrown into the Roman Mamertine prison. Here, Paul wrote 2 Timothy between AD 66 and 67. This was his deathbed epistle, before passing his legacy and the gospel baton to Timothy. Paul urged Timothy to bring to Rome his cloak, books, and parchments. He encouraged Timothy to remain strong and faithful in the face of opposition, persecutions, and suffering. Paul was executed by decapitation in AD 67.

Themes

2 Timothy was Paul's last letter before his martyrdom in the hands of Nero.

Paul encouraged Timothy to stay committed to Christ's Mission with urgency. He stressed the importance of perseverance, sound doctrine, and scripture.

Some of the main themes include the Christian's response to suffering, the gospel basis for endurance, the saving power of the gospel, and the danger of heretical doctrine.

Outline

2 Timothy 1:1–18, salutation, prayer, instructions

2 Timothy 2:1–26, passing the baton of faith, endure hardship, be a man of God

3:1–17, apostasy, heresy, Word of God

2 Timothy 4:1–22, preach the gospel, come before winter, farewell

Application

2 Timothy was Paul's last written document. He had done everything that he could for the Lord. He faced the prospect of brutal death. He had fought the great spiritual battle and run the marathon spiritual race of faith. The Christian faith is a super marathon relay race. Paul passed the gospel baton to Timothy, who in turn would pass it on to the next generation.

The gospel baton has passed from generation to generation for 2,000 years and is now in our hands. Our duty is to pass the gospel baton to the next generation for them to carry and pass it on to the next.

We are to pass the gospel baton of faith to our children and our children's children, by teaching, encouraging, conviction, correcting, and training them in godly and righteous living. We should not drop the baton that is in our hands!

Prayer

Heavenly Father, we pray for divine enablement and empowerment to pass the gospel baton of faith to our children. We pray for biblical literacy, biblical knowledge, and biblical education to prepare ourselves for this great undertaking. We pray for the salvation of our descendants. In Jesus' name, amen.

Chapter 9
Salutation, Prayer, Instructions

Prayer

Heavenly Father, may the words of our mouths and the thoughts of our hearts be acceptable to You. May You and the Holy Spirit's anointing be with us to open our spiritual eyes, ears, hearts, and minds to understand and apply Your teaching. In Jesus' name, amen.

2 Timothy 1:1–18

Verses 1–2, *1 Paul, an apostle of Jesus Christ through the will of God, according to the promise of the life which is in Christ Jesus, 2 to Timothy, my beloved child: Grace, mercy, and peace, from God the Father and Christ Jesus our Lord.*

Reflection

Paul spelled out his credentials: he was an apostle of Jesus Christ by the will of God according to the promise of God. Paul pronounced a blessing of grace, mercy, and peace on the recipient of this epistle, Timothy, his protégé and spiritual son in the faith.

Verses 3–7, *3 I thank God, whom I serve as my forefathers did, with a pure conscience. How unceasing is my memory of you in my petitions, night and day 4 longing to see you, remembering your tears, that I may be filled with joy; 5 having been reminded of the sincere faith that is in you, which lived first in your grandmother Lois, and your mother Eunice, and, I am persuaded, in you also. 6 For this cause, I remind you that you should stir up the gift of God which is in you through the laying on of my hands. 7 For God didn't give us a spirit of fear, but of power, love, and self-control.*

Reflection

Paul thanked God in prayer day and night without ceasing, with a pure conscience and a great desire to see Timothy. Timothy's messianic Christian grandmother, Lois, and mother, Eunice, nurtured him in the faith from a young age. Paul imparted spiritual gifts to Timothy through the laying on of hands. He encouraged Timothy to be bold because the indwelling Holy Spirit would anoint him with power and a sound mind.

Verses 8–11, *8 Therefore don't be ashamed of the testimony of our Lord, nor of me his prisoner; but endure hardship for the Good News according to the power of God, 9 who saved us and called us with a holy calling, not according to our works, but according to his own purpose and grace, which was given to us in Christ Jesus before times eternal, 10 but has now been revealed by the appearing of our Savior, Christ Jesus, who abolished death, and brought life and immortality to light through the Good News. 11 For this I was appointed as a preacher, an apostle, and a teacher of the Gentiles.*

Reflection

Paul encouraged Timothy to share in his sufferings, and not be ashamed of him or the gospel of Christ. The gospel had the power of God to save lives, Romans 1:16. God saved us with a Holy calling, not according to our works but according to His grace. He saved us by grace through faith. Jesus Christ through His incarnation abolished death on the cross and brought eternal life and immortality to those who believe in Him. Paul spelled out his credentials again: he was a preacher, apostle, and teacher to the Gentiles.

Romans 1:16, *For I am not ashamed of the gospel of Christ, for it is the power of God to salvation for everyone who believes, for the Jew first and also for the Greek.*

Verse 12, *For this cause I also suffer these things. Yet I am not ashamed, for I know him whom I have believed, and I am persuaded that he is able to guard that which I have committed to him against that day.*

Reflection

Despite suffering and persecutions, Paul was not ashamed of the gospel, because he believed that Christ was able to keep all that he had committed to Him until His second coming.

Verses 13–18, *13 Hold the pattern of sound words which you have heard from me, in faith and love which is in Christ Jesus. 14 That good thing which was committed to you, guard through the Holy Spirit who dwells in us. 15 This you know, that all who are in Asia turned away from me, of whom are Phygellus and Hermogenes. 16 May the Lord grant mercy to the house of Onesiphorus, for he often refreshed me, and was not ashamed of my chain, 17 but when he was in Rome, he sought me diligently and found me 18 (the Lord grant to him to find the Lord's mercy in that day); and in how many things he served at Ephesus, you know very well.*

Reflection

Paul encouraged Timothy to believe in sound doctrine with faith and love. Many of his supporters in Asia Minor including Phygellus and Hermogenes had deserted him. Paul prayed for the family of Onesiphorus, his faithful supporter and co-worker in the faith, who was not ashamed of him and ministered to him in many ways at Ephesus.

Application

Are you developing and using your spiritual gifts and callings effectively? Consider what God has gifted you and then find ways to use it for His glory. This could be through serving in the church, volunteering in your local community, or exploring training/educational opportunities that you are interested in.

You can better understand who God made you by exploring and reviewing your spiritual gifts and calls. These abilities can have a greater impact on church, community, and personal settings.

Believe in sound doctrines with faith and love. You must not be ashamed of the gospel despite suffering, tribulations, and persecutions, because it is the power of God to save lives. Persevere in prayer every day, giving thanks to God, and interceding for our family, friends, and associates.

Prayer

Heavenly Father, help us to hold firmly to sound doctrines with faith and love. Help us not t be ashamed of the gospel, because it has the power to save lives. Help us give thanks to You every day in prayer and intercession for our family, friends, and associates. In Jesus' name, amen.

Chapter 10

Pass the Baton of Faith

Prayer

Heavenly Father, we worship You in Spirit and in truth, giving You all the power, glory, honor, and praise. We bow at Your feet in reverence and awe. In Jesus' name, amen.

2 Timothy 2:1–26

Verses 1–2, *1 You therefore, my child, be strengthened in the grace that is in Christ Jesus. 2 The things which you have heard from me among many witnesses, commit the same things to faithful men, who will be able to teach others also.*

Reflection

Paul instructed Timothy to be strong in grace and teach all that he had learned from Paul to faithful men and women in the church who would in turn teach it to others. Timothy's task was to pass on the baton of faith through discipleship and training of faithful Christians.

Verses 3–7, *3 You therefore must endure hardship as a good soldier of Christ Jesus. 4 No soldier on duty entangles himself in the affairs of life, that he may please him who enrolled him as a soldier. 5 Also, if anyone competes in athletics, he isn't crowned unless he has competed by the rules. 6 The farmer who labors must be the first to get a share of the crops. 7 Consider what I say, and may the Lord give you understanding in all things.*

Reflection

Paul encouraged Timothy to endure as a soldier the hardship and suffering of the gospel, to run the spiritual race of faith as an athlete, and to work diligently in evangelism as a farmer. Timothy was to be as tough as a soldier, as disciplined as an athlete, and as hard-working as a farmer.

Verses 8–10, *8 Remember Jesus Christ, risen from the dead, of the offspring of David, according to my Good News, 9 in which I suffer hardship to the point of chains as a criminal. But God's word isn't chained. 10 Therefore I endure all things for the chosen ones' sake, that they also may obtain the salvation which is in Christ Jesus with eternal glory.*

Reflection

The gospel message is about the death, burial, resurrection, ascension, and glorification of Jesus Christ, a descendant of David. Paul was chained in the prison but the gospel was not chained to anything, anyone, or anywhere. Even prison could not stop the preaching and evangelism of the gospel. Paul endured all things so that whoever believed in Christ will be saved.

Verses 11–13, *11 This saying is trustworthy: "For if we died with him, we will also live with him. 12 If we endure, we will also reign with him. If we deny him, he also will deny us. 13 If we are faithless, he remains faithful; for he can't deny himself."*

Reflection

This may be a poem from antiquity. If we die with Christ, we will live with Him; if we endure hardship with Him, we will reign with Him; if we deny Him, He will deny us; if we are faithless, He will still be faithful.

Verses 14–15, *14 Remind them of these things, charging them in the sight of the Lord, that they don't argue about words, to no profit, to the subverting of those who hear. 15 Give diligence to present yourself approved by God, a workman who doesn't need to be ashamed, properly handling the Word of Truth.*

Reflection

Paul charged Timothy to present himself as an approved workman of God by teaching, preaching, and interpreting Scripture correctly and truthfully to convict, correct, encourage, and train his audience.

Verses 16–19, *16 But shun empty chatter, for it will go further in ungodliness, 17 and those words will consume like gangrene, of whom is Hymenaeus and Philetus: 18 men who have erred concerning the truth, saying that the resurrection is already past, and overthrowing the faith of some. 19 However God's firm foundation stands, having this seal, "The Lord knows those who are his, [Numbers 16:5]" and, "Let every one who names the name of the Lord depart from unrighteousness."*

Reflection

Paul instructed Timothy to run away from the worldly, empty, and ungodly talk that could spread like wildfire if left unchecked. Paul singled out by name two heretical teachers in the Ephesian church: Hymenaeus and Philetus, who claimed that the second coming of Christ had already come.

Verses 20–21, *20 Now in a large house there are not only vessels of gold and of silver, but also of wood and of clay. Some are for honor, and some for dishonor. 21 If anyone therefore purges himself from these, he will be a vessel for honor, sanctified, and suitable for the master's use, prepared for every good work.*

Reflection

In a house are vessels of gold and silver and vessels of wood and clay. The vessels of gold and silver speak of those who are sanctified, useful, and honorable to Christ. The vessels of wood and clay are those who are not sanctified, and are useless and dishonorable to Christ.

Verses 22–26, *22 Flee from youthful lusts; but pursue righteousness, faith, love, and peace with those who call on the Lord out of a pure heart. 23 But refuse foolish and ignorant questionings, knowing that they generate strife. 24 The Lord's servant must not quarrel, but be gentle toward all, able to teach, patient, 25 in gentleness correcting those who oppose him: perhaps God may give them repentance leading to a full knowledge of the truth, 26 and they may recover themselves out of the devil's snare, having been taken captive by him to his will.*

Reflection

Paul instructed Timothy to flee from youthful lusts, pursue righteousness with faith, love, and peace from a pure heart, to avoid quarreling over foolish and doubtful matters, to be gentle, patient, and humble in teaching the gospel of truth.

Application

Think about how you respond to challenges and difficulties. Do you face them with patience and faith or are you irritable and impulsive?

Develop a resilient spirit and rely on God to provide strength in difficult times. Find ways to support and encourage those who are facing similar challenges and support those who need your help.

Avoid youthful lusts, pursue righteousness, faith, love, and peace from a pure heart.

Avoid foolish disputes, be gentle, patient, and humble.

Correct, rebuke, convict, and teach others regarding the gospel of truth.

Prayer

Heavenly Father, we pray for Your empowerment to live our lives worthy of Your divine calling and election. Help us to pursue righteousness with faith, love, and peace from a pure heart. Help us to be gentle, patient, humble, and convict, correct, encourage, and teach the gospel of truth. In Jesus' name, amen.

Chapter 11
Apostasy, Heresy, Word of God

Prayer

Heavenly Father, thank You for the ministry of Your Word. We claim the promise that Your Word will accomplish its purpose and not return to You void, Isaiah 55:11. In Jesus' name, amen.

2 Timothy 3:1–17

Verses 1–5, *1 But know this: that in the last days, grievous times will come. 2 For men will be lovers of self, lovers of money, boastful, arrogant, blasphemers, disobedient to parents, unthankful, unholy, 3 without natural affection, unforgiving, slanderers, without self-control, fierce, not lovers of good, 4 traitors, headstrong, conceited, lovers of pleasure rather than lovers of God, 5 holding a form of godliness, but having denied its power. Turn away from these, also.*

Reflection

In the last days, difficult times will come and people will fall away from the faith. People will be lovers of themselves, lovers of money, boastful, arrogant, slanderous, defiant, ungrateful, unholy, unloving, without self-control, brutal, treacherous, unfriendly, pleasure-seeking, and ungodly.

Verses 6–9, *6 For some of these are people who creep into houses and take captive gullible women loaded down with sins, led away by various lusts, 7 always learning, and never able to come to the knowledge of the truth. 8 Even as Jannes and Jambres opposed Moses, so these also oppose the truth, men corrupted in mind, who concerning the faith are rejected. 9 But they will proceed no further. For their folly will be evident to all men, as theirs also came to be.*

Reflection

Ungodly men would come into houses to take advantage of and seduce gullible women. Jannes and Jambres, Pharaoh's magicians, could replicate some of the miracles of Moses, Exodus 7:11, 22; 8:7. Paul might have quoted non canonical sources in antiquity, as the names Jannes and Jambres are not found in the Old Testament. Just as Jannes and Jambres opposed Moses, these ungodly men opposed the truth of the gospel.

Exodus 7:11, *Pharaoh then summoned wise men and sorcerers, and the Egyptian magicians also did the same things by their secret arts.*

Exodus 7:22, *But the Egyptian magicians did the same things by their secret arts, and Pharaoh's heart became hard; he would not listen to Moses and Aaron, just as the Lord had said.*

Exodus 8:7, *But the magicians did the same things by their secret arts; they also made frogs come up on the land of Egypt.*

Verses 10–11, *10 But you followed my teaching, conduct, purpose, faith, patience, love, steadfastness, 11 persecutions, and sufferings: those things that happened to me at Antioch, Iconium, and Lystra. I endured those persecutions. The Lord delivered me out of them all.*

Reflection

Timothy was a godly man who followed Paul's doctrines with purpose, faith, love, and perseverance. Paul remembered his persecutions and afflictions from the hostile Jews at Antioch, Iconium, and Lystra and how the Lord had rescued him.

Verses 12–15, *12 Yes, and all who desire to live godly in Christ Jesus will suffer persecution. 13 But evil men and impostors will grow worse and worse, deceiving and being deceived. 14 But you remain in the things which you have learned and have been assured of, knowing from whom you have learned them. 15 From infancy, you have known the holy Scriptures which are able to make you wise for salvation through faith, which is in Christ Jesus.*

Reflection

Everyone who wants to live godly in Christ will suffer persecution from evil men and imposters. Timothy had to remain faithful to holy Scripture because it has the power to save those who believe in Christ.

Verses 16–17, *16 Every Scripture is God-breathed and profitable for teaching, for reproof, for correction, and for instruction in righteousness, 17 that each person who belongs to God may be complete, thoroughly equipped for every good work.*

Reflection

The Bible is written through God's inspiration and is useful for teaching, convicting, correcting, encouraging, training, and equipping Godly people in righteous living and doing God's work.

2 Peter 1:21, *for prophecy never came by the will of man, but holy men of God spoke as they were moved by the Holy Spirit.*

Application

Assess your relationship with Scripture. Commit to reading and applying the Bible in your everyday life. Bible study is important to better understand God's word. Share this truth with others for encouragement, teaching, or correction.

By reading and following Scripture, you can experience the transforming power of God's word. Study the Bible and let it guide you to a closer relationship with God and influence others' lives.

In the last days, false teachers will appear and many people will fall away from the faith. The godly will suffer persecutions at the hands of the Antichrist.

Continue to remain faithful to Christ and share the gospel. The acronym for "Basic Instructions Before Leaving Earth" is "BIBLE." Have a high view of Scripture and study it diligently.

Prayer

Heavenly Father, we pray for divine protection in the face of trials, tribulations, sufferings, and persecutions in the last days. We pray for Your divine assistance to remain strong in the faith and stay true to Your calling. In Jesus' name, amen.

Chapter 12
Farewell Address

Prayer

Heavenly Father, help us to be students, teachers, and preachers of Your Word. Help us to be ready to share our testimony, to teach, and preach the gospel in season and out of season. In Jesus' name, amen.

2 Timothy 4:1–22

Verses 1–2, *1 I command you therefore before God and the Lord Jesus Christ, who will judge the living and the dead at his appearing and his Kingdom: 2 preach the word; be urgent in season and out of season; reprove, rebuke, and exhort with all patience and teaching.*

Reflection

Greek for appearing is *epiphanes*, which refers to Christ's second coming. The two other Greeks words used for Christ's second coming in the Bible are *parousia*, which means being present, and *apokalypsis*, which means, *revelation*.

At His second coming, Christ will judge the living and the dead at the great white throne judgment, Revelation 20:11–12.

Paul charged Timothy to be ready to preach the word at any occasion, whenever and wherever an opportunity arose, and to convict, correct, encourage, and teach with patience.

Revelation 20:11–12, *Then I saw a great white throne and Him who sat on it, from whose face the earth and the heaven fled away. And there was found no place for them. And I saw the dead, small and great, standing before God, and books were opened. And another book was opened, which is the Book of Life. And the dead were judged according to their works, by the things which were written in the books.*

Verses 3–5, *3 For the time will come when they will not listen to the sound doctrine, but having itching ears, will heap up for themselves teachers after their own lusts, 4 and will turn away their ears from the truth, and turn away to fables. 5 But you be sober in all things, suffer hardship, do the work of an evangelist, and fulfill your ministry.*

Reflection

In the last days, people will not listen to sound doctrine. They will listen only to false teachers who will say what they want to hear. They will turn away from the truth and turn toward heresy. Paul encouraged Timothy to be vigilant, endure hardships, and evangelize to fulfill his God-ordained ministry.

Verses 6–8, *6 For I am already being offered, and the time of my departure has come. 7 I have fought the good fight. I have finished the course. I have kept the faith. 8 From now on, the crown of righteousness is stored up for me, which the Lord, the righteous judge, will give to me on that day; and not to me only, but also to all those who have loved his appearing.*

Reflection

In his goodbye address, Paul predicted that his life would end as a drink offering for God. He had fought the spiritual battle of faith and had run the spiritual race of faith. There was nothing more he could do except to wait for the crown of righteousness from Christ on the day of His second coming.

Verses 9–16, *9 Be diligent to come to me soon, 10 for Demas left me, having loved this present world, and went to Thessalonica; Crescens to Galatia; and Titus to Dalmatia. 11 Only Luke is with me. Take Mark, and bring him with you, for he is useful to me for service. 12 But I sent Tychicus to Ephesus. 13 Bring the cloak that I left at Troas with Carpus when you come, and the books, especially the parchments. 14 Alexander, the coppersmith, did much evil to me. The Lord will repay him according to his deeds, 15 of whom you also must beware; for he greatly opposed our words.16 At my first defense, no one came to help me, but all left me. May it not be held against them.*

Reflection

Paul singled out Demas, who had left the faith for the world. Paul singled out Alexander the coppersmith, who had betrayed him. He mentioned by name those who were faithful to him: Crescens, Titus, Luke, Mark, and Tychicus. He instructed Timothy to bring along John Mark, and Paul's books and cloak. John Mark was the writer of the Gospel of Mark and cousin of Barnabas. He had abandoned Paul on his first missionary journey but Paul had reconciled with him.

Verses 17–18, *17 But the Lord stood by me and strengthened me, that through me the message might be fully proclaimed, and that all the Gentiles might hear. So I was delivered out of the mouth of the lion. 18 And the Lord will deliver me from every evil work, and will preserve me for his heavenly Kingdom. To him be the glory forever and ever. Amen.*

Reflection

The Lord was with Paul, strengthening, protecting, and preserving him for His heavenly kingdom. Paul gave glory to Christ in a doxology.

Verses 19–21, *19 Greet Prisca and Aquila, and the house of Onesiphorus. 20 Erastus remained at Corinth, but I left Trophimus at Miletus sick. 21 Be diligent to come before winter. Eubulus salutes you, as do Pudens, Linus, Claudia, and all the brothers.*

Reflection

Paul acknowledged and mentioned by name Prisca, Aquila, the family of Onesiphorus, Erastus, Trophimus, Eubulus, Pudens, Linus, and Claudia.

Verse 22, *22 The Lord Jesus Christ be with your spirit. Grace be with you. Amen.*

Reflection

In closing, Paul pronounced a blessing of grace on Timothy from the Lord Jesus Christ.

Application

Consider your readiness to share the Gospel. Prepare yourself to share your faith at any time; be alert for opportunities to discuss it with others. Prepare yourself by reading the scriptures, praying for guidance and practicing your testimony in public. Share with patience and kindness, as it is an act that is done out of love and service.

Remember to be attentive and empathic when you share your faith. This can lead to meaningful conversations while removing any misconceptions about the gospel message.

Sharing your faith requires a heart filled with compassion and a willingness to listen to others. By approaching conversations with empathy and understanding, you can create a space for genuine connection and spiritual growth.

Time is running out. Preach the Word of God in season and out of season. Do the work of an evangelist to share the gospel whenever and wherever there is an opportunity.

Prayer

Heavenly Father, help us to be diligent students and teachers of Your Word. Help us to be ready to teach and preach Your Word in season and out of season to anyone, anywhere, and at any time. In Jesus' name, amen.

Chapter 13
Introduction to Titus

In his letter to Titus, Paul offered guidance for church leadership and godly living. Paul emphasized the significance of teaching correct beliefs, living according to the teachings of the gospel, and performing good deeds.

Prayer

Heavenly Father, we pray for Your Living Bread, Living Manna, Living Water, and Living Word of Eternal Life to nourish, strengthen, sustain, quench, and nurture our souls. In Jesus' name, amen.

Author, Date, Recipient, Setting

After his release from his first Roman imprisonment but before his rearrest to serve his second Roman imprisonment in AD 66, the apostle Paul wrote the epistle of Titus from an unknown location to a person in Crete named Titus, between AD 63 and 65. Paul wrote a personal pastoral letter to Titus, his protégé and spiritual son in the faith, to help him lead the churches in the Crete.

Crete

Ancient Crete, modern-day Kriti or Candia, is one of the largest islands in the Mediterranean. Ancient Crete was prosperous and had a large thriving population, but Cretans were notorious for their immorality. The Cretan poet Epimenides said, "all Cretans are liars, evil beasts, lazy gluttons," Titus 1:12.

Themes

The main themes are the relationships between faith and practice, belief and behavior, truth and heresy, instructions for Christian living, and the criteria for selecting church leaders.

Purpose

After release from his first Roman imprisonment, Paul visited Crete. He left Titus in Crete to oversee the churches he had planted. He advised Titus to reject the heretical Gnostics and Judaizers, Titus 1:10, 14. This "circumcision party" had insisted that Gentile Christians believe in Jewish myths, keep the Mosaic law, and undergo circumcision. Paul instructed Titus on Christian living, selection of elders and bishops, and to reject heresy,

Outline

Titus 1:1–16, salutation, criteria for selecting elders/bishops, rejecting false teachers

Titus 2:1–16, Christian relationships

Titus 3:1–15, submit to authorities, avoid foolish disputes, farewell

Application

The epistle of Titus transcends time. Paul's instructions, encouragements, and teachings to Titus also apply to us. Sadly, heretical doctrines from the first-century church have continued into our own day. We must be able to discern and reject the deviant teachings so rampant today.

Prayer

Heavenly Father, teach us Your doctrines. May we walk away from here refreshed and renewed. We acknowledge that Your Word is Holy and True and is powerful to save lives. May we remain in You, and may Your Word remain in us. In Jesus' name, amen.

Chapter 14
Salutation, Selecting Elders/ Bishops

Prayer

Heavenly Father, thank You for inspiring the writings of the apostle Paul that transcend time and culture. Thank You for the life of an apostle *par excellence* to the Gentiles. In Jesus' name, amen.

Titus 1:1–16

Verses 1–4, *1 Paul, a servant of God, and an apostle of Jesus Christ, according to the faith of God's chosen ones, and the knowledge of the truth which is according to godliness, 2 in hope of eternal life, which God, who can't lie, promised before time began; 3 but in his own time revealed his word in the message with which I was entrusted according to the commandment of God our Savior; 4 to Titus, my true child according to a common faith: Grace, mercy, and peace from God the Father and the Lord Jesus Christ our Savior.*

Reflection

Paul spelled out his credentials: he was a slave of God, an apostle of Jesus Christ, and one of God's elect. God, who cannot lie, promised in eternity past a Savior, who came in the flesh through the incarnation of Jesus Christ, the Word of God. Paul committed himself to preach the gospel of Christ. Paul pronounced a greeting of grace, mercy, and peace on Titus from God and the Lord Jesus Christ

Verses 5–9, *5 I left you in Crete for this reason, that you would set in order the things that were lacking and appoint elders in every city, as I directed you, 6 if anyone is blameless, the husband of one wife, having children who believe, who are not accused of loose or unruly behavior. 7 For the overseer must be blameless, as God's steward, not self-pleasing, not easily angered, not given to wine, not violent, not greedy for dishonest gain; 8 but given to hospitality, a lover of good, sober minded, fair, holy, self-controlled, 9 holding to the faithful word which is according to the teaching, that he may be able to exhort in the sound doctrine, and to convict those who contradict him.*

Reflection

"Elder," *presbyteros*, and "bishop," *episkopos*, refer to the same office, that of overseer. Paul spelled out the qualifications of an elder/bishop. He must be male and be above reproach, the husband of one wife, and have faithful children. He must not be self-willed or quick tempered, but abstain from wine, be gentle, not be greedy for money, be hospitable, sober, just, holy, self-controlled, faithful to the Word, and able to teach sound doctrine to encourage, convict, and correct.

Verses 10–16, *10 For there are also many unruly men, vain talkers and deceivers, especially those of the circumcision, 11 whose mouths must be stopped: men who overthrow whole houses, teaching things which they ought not, for dishonest gain's sake. 12 One of them, a prophet of their own, said, "Cretans are always liars, evil beasts, and idle gluttons." 13 This testimony is true. For this cause, reprove them sharply, that they may be sound in the faith, 14 not paying attention to Jewish fables and commandments of men who turn away from the truth. 15 To the pure, all things are pure; but to those who are defiled and unbelieving, nothing is pure; but both their mind and their conscience are defiled. 16 They profess that they know God, but by their deeds they deny him, being abominable, disobedient, and unfit for any good work.*

Reflection

"Those of the circumcision" were the Judaizers, legalistic, heretical teachers who peddled the teaching of Jewish myths, Mosaic law, circumcision, and Jewish rituals. Paul rebuked them for abusing the gospel for dishonest monetary gain and for lying. He also rebuked the Cretans for their laziness and gluttony. Paul said that to the pure everything is pure, but to the impure nothing is pure because of a defiled conscience. These people, who professed to know God, denied His existence by what they did!

Application

Reflect on your own leadership qualities, whether in the church, at work, or in your family. Do you possess the traits that Paul describes? Strive to develop qualities such as integrity, self-control, and faithfulness in all areas of your life.

Support and encourage those who are in leadership roles, praying for their wisdom and guidance. As you reflect on your own leadership qualities, it is important to examine whether you embody the traits Paul describes.

It's important to always work on qualities like integrity, self-control, and faithfulness in all areas of your life, so you can set a good example. It's important to support and encourage leaders and pray for their wisdom and guidance, as they have a significant impact on the growth and well-being of communities.

Not all teachers teach sound doctrines. Be able to discern and reject heretical doctrines. Avoid idle talking, abusing the gospel for monetary gain, legalism, dishonesty, laziness, and gluttony.

Congregations should follow Paul's criteria for selecting elders.

Prayer

Heavenly Father, we pray for wisdom to discern and reject heretical doctrines and heretical teachers. Protect us from deceptions, thieves, and scammers. In Jesus' name, amen.

Chapter 15
Christian Relationships

Titus 2:1–16

Verses 1–5, *1 But say the things which fit sound doctrine, 2 that older men should be temperate, sensible, sober minded, sound in faith, in love, and in perseverance: 3 and that older women likewise be reverent in behavior, not slanderers nor enslaved to much wine, teachers of that which is good, 4 that they may train the young wives to love their husbands, to love their children, 5 to be sober minded, chaste, workers at home, kind, being in subjection to their own husbands, that God's word may not be blasphemed.*

Reflection

Paul spelled out proper Christian relationships according to sound doctrine. The older men should not be drunk with wine, but be respectful, calm, faithful, loving, and patient. The older women should be respectful, not slanderers, and not be drunk with wine. They should teach younger women to love their husbands and children and be good, discreet, chaste, and obedient housewives.

Verses 6–10, *6 Likewise, exhort the younger men to be sober minded. 7 In all things show yourself an example of good works. In your teaching, show integrity, seriousness, incorruptibility, 8 and soundness of speech that can't be condemned, that he who opposes you may be ashamed, having no evil thing to say about us. 9 Exhort servants to be in subjection to their own masters and to be well-pleasing in all things, not contradicting, 10 not stealing, but showing all good fidelity, that they may adorn the doctrine of God, our Savior, in all things.*

Reflection

Young men should not be drunk with wine, but be above reproach in character, sound in doctrine, respectful, incorruptible, and graceful in speech. Slaves should obey their masters and not pilfer their goods.

Verses 11–15, *11 For the grace of God has appeared, bringing salvation to all men, 12 instructing us to the intent that, denying ungodliness and worldly lusts, we would live soberly, righteously, and godly in this present age; 13 looking for the blessed hope and appearing of the glory of our great God and Savior, Jesus Christ, 14 who gave himself for us, that he might redeem us from all iniquity, and purify for himself a people for his own possession, zealous for good works. 15 Say these things and exhort and reprove with all authority. Let no one despise you.*

Reflection

People are saved by the grace of God. Christians should stay away from ungodliness and lust, not be drunk with wine, and live righteous and godly lives in the present age, while anticipating the second coming of Christ. As already mentioned, Greek for "appearing" is *epiphanes*, which means manifest or become visible. The glorious appearing of Christ speaks of His second coming. Christ gave Himself for us on the cross to redeem us from sin. Paul exhorted Titus to encourage and correct the people under his care with authority and allow no one to despise him.

Application

Evaluate the teachings that you share and follow. Are they based on sound doctrine? Study the Scriptures closely to ensure that your beliefs and teachings are in line with them. Encourage and mentor others to spread good doctrine by being a godly example.

In order to maintain sound doctrine, it is essential that you keep an open mind when it comes to your beliefs and teachings. You can align your teachings and beliefs with the Bible by studying Scripture and helping others.

Think about areas of your life that may show ungodliness or worldliness, and lead a self-controlled and upright life. Assess your choices, habits and relationships to ensure they are in line with godly living. This may include setting boundaries or seeking accountability.

Do not be drunk with wine, but be respectful, calm, faithful, loving, and patient.

Be above reproach in character, sound in our doctrine, and graceful in your speech.

Christian employees should obey their employers and not pilfer their goods.

Live righteous and godly lives.

Prayer

Heavenly Father, we acknowledge that Scripture is Your inspired, infallible, and inerrant Word to us. Sanctify us by Your Word of truth so that we will know the truth and the truth will set us free. In Jesus' name, amen.

Chapter 16
Farewell Address

Titus 3:1–15

Verses 1–3, *1 Remind them to be in subjection to rulers and to authorities, to be obedient, to be ready for every good work, 2 to speak evil of no one, not to be contentious, to be gentle, showing all humility toward all men. 3 For we were also once foolish, disobedient, deceived, serving various lusts and pleasures, living in malice and envy, hateful, and hating one another.*

Reflection

Christians should submit to authorities and rulers, be obedient, not speak evil of others, be peaceful, gentle, and humble, remembering that we were once foolish, disobedient, deceiving, lustful, malicious, envious, and hateful.

Verses 4–7, *4 But when the kindness of God our Savior and his love toward mankind appeared, 5 not by works of righteousness which we did ourselves, but according to his mercy, he saved us through the washing of regeneration and renewing by the Holy Spirit, 6 whom he poured out on us richly, through Jesus Christ our Savior; 7 that being justified by his grace, we might be made heirs according to the hope of eternal life.*

Reflection

People are saved not by doing good works but by Christ's mercy and grace, through the washing of the Word of God and regeneration of the Holy Spirit. People are saved and justified by grace through faith in Jesus Christ. When people believe in the finished work of Christ on the cross, they are regenerated or born again and adopted as heirs of God.

Verse 8, *This saying is faithful, and concerning these things I desire that you affirm confidently, so that those who have believed God may be careful to maintain good works. These things are good and profitable to men.*

Reflection

Good works are not a prerequisite of salvation but the result of salvation. Faith in Christ is a prerequisite of salvation. Good works are our response to God's grace, mercy, and love.

Verses 9–11, *9 but shun foolish questionings, genealogies, strife, and disputes about the law; for they are unprofitable and vain. 10 Avoid a factious man after a first and second warning, 11 knowing that such a one is perverted and sins, being self-condemned.*

Reflection

Christians should avoid disputes on doubtful matters, genealogies, and legalism. Christians should reject argumentative and disruptive people after going through the due process of admonition.

Verses 12–14, *12 When I send Artemas to you, or Tychicus, be diligent to come to me to Nicopolis, for I have determined to winter there. 13 Send Zenas, the lawyer, and Apollos on their journey speedily, that nothing may be lacking for them. 14 Let our people also learn to maintain good works for necessary uses, that they may not be unfruitful.*

Reflection

Paul would be sending Artemis or Tychicus to Titus in Crete. Paul wanted to meet Titus in Nicopolis in the winter.

Verse 15, *All who are with me greet you. Greet those who love us in faith. Grace be with you all. Amen.*

In his farewell address, Paul pronounced a blessing of grace on Titus.

Application

Evaluate your involvement in debates or arguments. Do you find yourself getting involved in counterproductive disputes? Focus on what's important and avoid unproductive conflicts within the faith community. Engage in productive, respectful discussions while seeking peace and unity.

Assess your commitment to doing good. Do you take proactive measures to meet the needs of others? Find ways to help and support those who need it, whether that is through church events or community service initiatives. Be fruitful with your good deeds to leave a positive impact on others.

Submit to authorities and rulers, be obedient, peaceful, gentle, and humble, remembering that you too were once foolish, disobedient, deceitful, lustful, malicious, envious, and hateful.

Salvation is by grace through faith in Christ. Salvation is by grace, through faith in Christ, and not by works. Good work is our response to Christ's grace, mercy, and love to us.

Prayer

Heavenly Father, thank You for giving us the strength and perseverance to complete 1 Timothy, 2 Timothy, and Titus. Thank You for Your timely Word that transcends culture and time. We pray for wisdom to understand and apply Scripture in our daily living. In Jesus' name, amen.

About the Author

Dr Andrew C S Koh is a retired cardiologist, Bible teacher, and author of 55 titles. With a passion for making Scripture come alive, he blends theological insight with practical life application to help readers grow in faith and understanding. His writing reflects a deep commitment to God's Word, forged through decades of medical service, spiritual study, and personal devotion. Dr. Koh's works have encouraged believers around the world to walk closer with Christ and live out their calling with purpose and conviction.

Koh's unique perspective blends his extensive knowledge of the medical field with his deep theological insights. He studied theology at Laidlaw College in Auckland, New Zealand. He now calls Malaysia home, where he lives with his family. He made history in 2021 by setting a record in the Malaysia Book of Records for publishing the most books in a single year.

Whether he's teaching the Bible, creating digital content, or sharing his thoughts through various media, Dr. Koh's mission is clear: to make the Word of God accessible and relevant to everyday life. His works aim to inspire believers to grow deeper in their faith, live with purpose, and embrace the transformative power of God's love.

Author of From Stethoscope to Wisdom

https://books.drandrewcskoh.com/link-tree

https://storyoriginapp.com/giveaways/a517155c-75a2-11ef-a813-bbd0e34c8b27

Link Tree:

https://linktr.ee/andrewcskoh

Universal book link:

https://books2read.com/ap/xX066D/Dr-Andrew-C-S-Koh

New Release Notification:

https://books2read.com/author/dr-andrew-c-s-koh/subscribe/1/384961/

Free Book:

https://storyoriginapp.com/giveaways/b295be58-7736-11ec-ac4b-e34d930c508e

One Last Thing

Thank you for selecting my book. I genuinely hope it has offered you an enjoyable and stimulating experience. I would appreciate your feedback and would be grateful if you could write a review on the platform where you bought it or on a book review site. Your feedback will help others make choices and show me which parts of the book were effective or lacking. Your honest review will help me grow as a writer and motivate me to create more engaging stories in the future.

Thank you once again for taking the time to explore my book. I genuinely hope it proved to be a rewarding experience for you. Your support means everything to me, and I am truly grateful to each reader who joins me on this journey. Together, we can cultivate a vibrant community of readers and writers united by our love for storytelling.

Each review contributes to a vibrant dialogue that enriches our literary experience. I look forward to hearing your thoughts and insights as we continue to explore the depths of creativity together. Your feedback is invaluable, and it inspires me to keep pushing the boundaries of my writing. Let's keep the conversation going and delve deeper into the stories that connect us all.

Dr Andrew C S Koh

Scan the QR code to get a free audiobook

Don't miss out!

Visit the website below and you can sign up to receive emails whenever Dr Andrew C S Koh publishes a new book. There's no charge and no obligation.

https://books2read.com/r/B-A-FMXV-MYFDC

Did you love *Pastoral Epistles: 1 Timothy, 2 Timothy, Titus*? Then you should read *From Love to Light*[1] by Dr Andrew C S Koh!

Discover the Depth of God's Love and the Clarity of His Light.

Are you ready to go deeper in your walk with Christ?

From Love to Light: Exploring 1, 2, 3 John, and Jude is a transformative Bible study and devotional designed for personal or group use. With clarity and pastoral warmth, this book walks you through the powerful themes of love, truth, obedience, and assurance in the Epistles of John. The epistle of Jude is added as an additional bonus to the readers.

Each chapter includes:

Clear, verse-by-verse commentary

Reflective questions for personal growth

Group discussion prompts

Practical applications for everyday living

---

1. https://books2read.com/u/me6gGz

2. https://books2read.com/u/me6gGz

Whether you're a seasoned believer or new to Bible study, this book will help you move from simply knowing about God's love to living daily in His light. Read more at https://www.drandrewcskoh.com.

Also by Dr Andrew C S Koh

Bible Study
From Creation to Covenant
From Deceiver to Destiny: Jacob's Story
From Slavery to Freedom
From Man to Mission
From Slave to Brother
From Symbols to Salvation
From Legalism to Liberty
From Tribulation to Triumph

Daily Devotion
Manna of Life: Daily Devotion

Daily Devotions
Bread of Life Daily Devotions
Words of Eternal Life
Bread From Heaven: Daily Devotions
Light of the World Daily Devotions
Light of the World Daily Devotions
The Way, the Truth, and the Life
Rooted: A Daily Devotion to Deepen your Faith

Fiction
The Hourglass Paradox

Genesis
Understanding Genesis 1-11: From Adam to Abraham
Faith Journey of Abraham: Genesis 12-25
Life Story of Jacob: Genesis 26-36
The Story of Joseph: Genesis 37-50
From Pit to Palace

Gospels and Act
The Gospel According to Matthew
Daily Devotion Gospel of Mark
The Gospel According to Luke
Daily Devotion Gospel of John
Acts: Volume 1 and 2, From Jerusalem to Rome
From Galilee to Golgotha

Non Pauline and General Epistles
Hebrews: the Just Shall Live by Faith
1 John, 2 John, 3 John & Jude: a Verse by Verse Bible Study
General Epistles: 1 Peter, 2 Peter, James

Pauline Epistles
Romans: The Just Shall Live by Faith
1 Corinthians
2 Corinthians

1 Thessalonians, 2 Thessalonians, Philemon
Pastoral Epistles: 1 Timothy, 2 Timothy, Titus
Galatians: Justified by Faith in Jesus Christ
Philemon: Charge to the Master's Account

Prison Epistles
The Prison Epistles
Philippians: Rejoice Always in the Lord
Colossians: He is the Image of the Invisible God
Ephesians: Every Spiritual Blessing in the Heavenly Places in Christ

Reflective Poems
Journey in Ryhme: Poems of Reflection
Whispers of Grace

Standalone
Apocalypse: Understanding the Book of Revelation
Expository Preaching
Memoirs of a Doctor
Moses: Let My People Go
Living Word Living Savior: a Portrait of Jesus Through the Eyes of John
From Stethoscope to Wisdom
Walking in His Footsteps: A Pilgrim's Journey
Mapping the Heart
The Forgotten Melody
Footprints in Time
From Love to Light
Time Traveller's Return

Watch for more at https://www.drandrewcskoh.com.

About the Author

Dr Andrew C S Koh a retired cardiologist, Bible teacher, and author of 50 titles. With a passion for making Scripture come alive, he blends theological insight with practical life application to help readers grow in faith and understanding. His writing reflects a deep commitment to God's Word, forged through decades of medical service, spiritual study, and personal devotion. Dr. Koh's works have encouraged believers around the world to walk closer with Christ and live out their calling with purpose and conviction.

Koh's unique perspective blends his extensive knowledge of the medical field with his deep theological insights. He studied theology at Laidlaw College in Auckland, New Zealand. He now calls Malaysia home, where he lives with his family. He made history in 2021 by setting a record in the Malaysia Book of Records for publishing the most books in a single year.

Whether he's teaching the Bible, creating digital content, or sharing his thoughts through various media, Dr. Koh's mission is clear: to make the Word of God accessible and relevant to everyday life. His works aim to inspire believers to grow deeper in their faith, live with purpose, and embrace the transformative power of God's love.

Link tree:

https://linktr.ee/andrewcskoh

https://books.drandrewcskoh.com/link-tree

free ebook:

https://storyoriginapp.com/giveaways/b295be58-7736-11ec-ac4b-e34d930c508e

Read more at https://www.drandrewcskoh.com.

About the Publisher

Dr. Andrew C. S. Koh is an independent publisher with an impressive portfolio of over 40 titles to his name. His works span a wide array of genres, showcasing his versatility and passion for diverse forms of writing. These genres include fiction, where he weaves captivating narratives, and non-fiction, where he explores a variety of thought-provoking subjects. Additionally, Dr. Koh has contributed to the literary world with insightful biographies and memoirs that offer deep reflections on personal journeys and historical figures.

His poetry resonates with readers through its emotional depth and eloquence, while his travel writings transport audiences to far-off destinations, sharing unique perspectives and experiences. Moreover, Dr. Koh has an extensive collection of works in the realms of Bible study and devotionals, offering spiritual guidance and inspiration to those seeking to deepen their faith. With each book, Dr. Koh has made a significant impact on the literary community, enriching readers' lives with his diverse and thoughtful publications..

Read more at https://www.drandrewcskoh.com.